LUNCH LADY SCIENCE

Understanding the Food that Goes in Your Body

By Darlene R. Stille

COMPASS POINT BOOKS
a capstone imprint

Compass Point Books
151 Good Counsel Drive
P.O. Box 669
Mankato, MN 56002-0669

Editors: Sarah Eason and Geoff Barker
Designers: Paul Myerscough and Geoff Ward
Media Researcher: Susannah Jayes
Content Consultant: Harold Pratt, President, Educational Consultants Inc.
and Science Curriculum Inc.
Production Specialist: Laura Manthe

Image Credits
Alamy: Robert Esposti 33, Fancy 29, GoGo Images Corporation 6b, Lucie Lang 26b, PCN
Photography 13; **Corbis:** Tomas Rodriguez 11b; **Capstone Studio/Karon Dubke:** cover, 8, 9,
16, 17, 30, 31, 40, 41, 44, 45, 55, 57; **Geoff Ward:** 34–35, 58r; **Photolibrary:** Image100 51;
Shutterstock: Martin Allinger 10b, argus 37, Tray Berry 52b, Tom Burlison 24b, Tony Campbell
32tl, 34tl, 36tl, 38tl, Cogipix 23r, Alistair Cotton 1, Tomas del Amo 18b, Bairachnyi Dmitry 5b,
East 48tl, 50tl, 52tl, FXQuadro 4tl, 6tl, 10tl Gemenacom 39, Jose Gil 5t, 20tr, 49r, Gorilla 14b,
Happydancing 59, Icons Jewellery 32br, ifong 27, Jezper 38tr, Jordache 63, Jan Kaliciak 24tl,
26tl, 28tl, Sebastian Kaulitzki 53t, Sebastien Knight 42b, Max Krasnov 3, Lasse Kristensen 50b,
53b, Tamara Kulikova back cover, 56tl, 58tl, 60tl, Jin Young Lee 60b, Robyn Mackenzie 28br,
Marema 23l, Morgan Lane Photography 7, Oksix 25, 46b, Fedorov Oleksiy 19t, Orientaly 47,
Pashapixel 60tr, Picsfive 12b, 58bl, Andrejs Pidjass 21, Photobar 15, Scott Sanders 61, Vladimir
Sazonov 56b, John Schwegel 19b, Jason Stitt 20bl, Piotr Tomicki 12tl, 14tl, 18tl, 20tl, 22tl,
Suzanne Tucker 42tl, 46tl, Ustyujanin 22b, Simone van den Berg 34bl, Sandra van der Steen
28bl, GraÃ§a Victoria 36br, Voronin 76 48–49, Amy Walters 11t, XAOC 14c, Igor Zh. 43.

Library of Congress Cataloging-in-Publication Data
Stille, Darlene R.
  Lunch lady science: understanding the food that goes in your body /
by Darlene R. Stille.
       p. cm.—(Everyday science)
  Includes bibliographical references and index.
  ISBN 978-0-7565-4484-3 (library binding)
  ISBN 978-0-7565-4502-4 (paperback)
  1. Food—Juvenile literature. 2. Nutrition—Juvenile literature. I. Title.
  TX355.S75 2012
  641.3—dc23   2011015248

Visit Compass Point Books on the Internet at *www.capstonepub.com*

Printed in the United States of America in Stevens Point, Wisconsin.
032011
006111WZF11

table of contents

why not pizza and fries every day?

Another lunch hour in the school cafeteria. Another day of the Lunch Lady serving milk, meat, and veggies. What'll it be—broccoli, carrots, corn, peas, or Brussels sprouts? What kid hasn't wondered: "Why can't we have pizza and fries for lunch every day?"

Nutritious Ingredients

So much choice. The Lunch Lady serves up a range of various foods—milk, meat, fruits, and vegetables. The foods contain a huge variety of nutrients—special kinds of chemicals that you need to help you get through a day of school. Protein, fats, and sugars and other carbohydrates are nutrients, as are vitamins and minerals.

Meat and milk are full of protein. Rice and potatoes are rich in carbohydrates. Vegetables and fruits are packed with all sorts of vitamins and minerals. The nutrients are fuel for your body and help keep your body in top shape. They give you energy to read books, figure out math problems, exercise in gym class, and play sports after school. Nutritious foods also help prevent certain diseases and help your body heal if you get sick or suffer an injury. A lot of thinking goes into the Lunch Lady's menu. Food experts plan a menu that contains food from each of the major food groups.

true tales

Housebound Teenager

Billy Robbins, of Houston, Texas, weighed 840 pounds (381 kilograms) by the time he was 18. Morbidly obese, he only ate pizzas, donuts, and burgers, and all he did was play computer games and sleep. Robbins could barely move, so he could not burn off all of the food he ate every day. He became housebound. With his health failing, he had to have surgery to lose weight. First Robbins went on a strict diet. Surgeons then made his stomach much smaller so that he couldn't eat as much. After surgery Robbins weighed 350 pounds (159 kilograms) less than when he arrived at the hospital.

Pizza again?!

You need to eat lots of different foods every day to give your body the nutrients it needs. So widen your menu to include more than just pizza!

The Major Food Groups

The grain group contains anything made from wheat, rice, oats, cornmeal, or other cereal grain. Breads, cereals, rice, crackers, pasta—and even pizza crust—are part of the grain group. Grains contain carbohydrates that your body uses for energy. Dieticians say you should eat about 6 ounces (170 grams) of grains each day.

There are two kinds of grain products, those made from whole grains and those made from refined grains. Refined grains go through a mill that takes out rough parts, called bran and germ. Bran is a part of the grain husk, the dry outer covering. Germ is the part of a seed that grows into a plant.

Junk food
is for losers!
Not me!

Don't Forget!

You also need the mineral calcium in milk and protein in fish, meat, and poultry. Try to have 3 cups of milk every day. Food scientists say you need about 6 ounces (170 grams) of meat, fish, poultry, or beans a day.

Fuel your body for sports with energy-giving carbohydrates, such as rice and bread. Build up muscle with protein-packed foods, such as meat, fish, and beans.

6

Food experts say that you should eat a variety of foods every day to provide your body with vital nutrients.

Whole grains contain the bran and germ. Refining grains removes fiber and certain vitamins. Fiber helps move food through your body. Food experts say you should eat whole grains whenever you can.

Vegetables and fruits are two other important food groups. These colorful foods are packed with vitamins and minerals. How much do you need? Eat 2½ cups of vegetables a day, especially such leafy green veggies as spinach and broccoli and such orange-colored veggies as carrots and sweet potatoes. And eat 2 cups of fruit a day. Eating fresh or frozen fruit is better than drinking fruit juice. By eating fruit rather than drinking juice, you take in more fiber and fill up faster.

Glue from Milk

The same chemicals that combine to make foods can be added together in various ways to make other products. In this experiment you will see how milk, vinegar, and baking soda combine to make glue.

You will need:

- Measuring cup
- Milk
- 2 small paper or plastic cups
- White vinegar
- Measuring spoon
- Spoon
- Cheesecloth
- Baking soda
- 2 narrow strips of paper

1. Measure out ¼ cup of milk and pour it into one of the paper or plastic cups.

2. Measure out 1 tablespoon of white vinegar and add it to the milk.

3. Stir the milk and vinegar for about 1 minute and watch the mixture change. Clumps called curds form in a clear liquid called whey. This is the way cheese is made. The curds become cheese.

4. Place the cheesecloth over the second cup and slowly pour the curds and whey into the cloth. The whey will go into the cup and the curds will stay in the cheesecloth.

5. Return the curds to the now-empty first cup. Add ¼ teaspoon baking soda and stir well to make a gluelike paste.

6. Spread the paste onto the ends of the paper strips. Fold the ends together so that they stick together to form loops. If you loop the loops together, you can make a paper chain.

By adding one ingredient, you made glue instead of cheese.

Super-Size the Celery, Please

Can you imagine pushing your tray along the school cafeteria line and asking the Lunch Lady to super-size your veggie serving? Yeah, right! But what happens at the fast food place? Fast food restaurants are making portions bigger—and people are getting bigger too. Three times as many kids were obese in 2008 as in 1980. Many kids eat too much and exercise too little. Other factors play a role, but the bottom line is this—if you want to lose weight, eat fewer calories than you burn each day.

Keep moving!

Try to fit some activity into your daily routine. You don't have to run a marathon—dancing, walking, and riding your bike all count as calorie busting exercise!

Cut Down on Fats and Sugars

You don't need a lot of fats or sugars. French fries and other fried foods contain much more fat than baked or boiled foods. Butter, margarine, and lard contain solid fats that can clog your arteries. Fats in olive oil, vegetable oil, nuts, and lean meat are better for keeping your heart healthy. Sodas, candy, cakes, pies, and other sweets are loaded with sugar. The sugar in these foods can cause tooth decay. Some sugary foods and drinks have empty calories—calories with little or no nutritional value. Eating or drinking too much of these means that you can quickly pile on weight.

Chocolate is full of fat and sugar, so keep it as a treat that you eat occasionally rather than all the time.

FACT!

What's BMI?

Body mass index (BMI) is a better measure than weight of whether a person is normal weight, overweight, or obese. BMI shows the amount of fat in your body. Health professionals figure it out using your height, weight, age, and gender.

is ketchup a vegetable?

Want a "balanced" meal with French fries as a carb, fried pork rinds as a protein, and tomato ketchup as a vegetable? Right, it's not good. French fries are carbs, but they also have lots of fat. Pork rinds may have some protein, but they, too, are chock-full of fats and salt. Ketchup has some good nutrients, but it is also full of sugar.

Store shelves and cases are packed with all types of food. How do you know which to choose? It takes some thought and planning to create meals that are good for you. What do all these nutrients do anyway?

Ketchup is packed with nutritious tomatoes, but it is also loaded with sugar. Don't overdo it when you add ketchup to your food.

Go easy on the ketchup!

What Does Protein Do?

Protein is one of the most important building blocks of your body. Proteins are big, complex molecules. Your muscles, skin, hair, and even your fingernails are made of protein. Molecules called enzymes, which speed up chemical reactions in your cells, are made of protein. Hormones that start important processes in your body are made of proteins, as are parts of your immune system, which fights disease.

Proteins are made up of tiny chemical units called amino acids. Your body needs 20 different amino acids to create various proteins. Your body can make 11 of them. The others, called essential amino acids, come from protein-rich foods—meat, fish, cheese, eggs, and milk.

What Do Carbs Do?

Carbs in your body are like the gas in a car engine. Along with fats and protein, your body depends upon carbs for energy. Food scientists measure the energy contained in foods in units called calories.

Candy bars, bagels, donuts, hamburger buns, and spaghetti are full of carbs. All of these foods come from plants. There are two kinds of carbs: simple carbs and complex carbs.

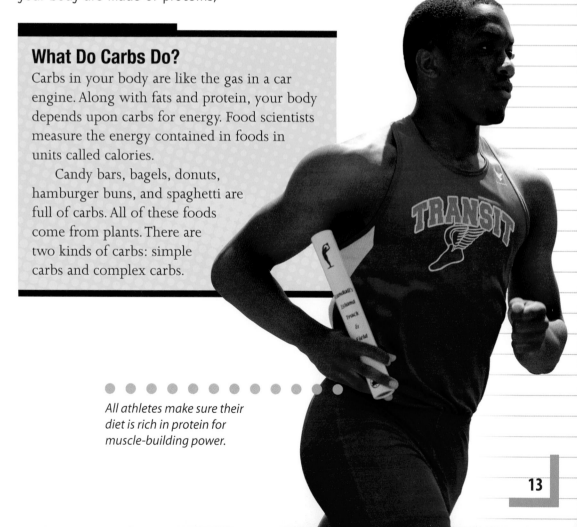

All athletes make sure their diet is rich in protein for muscle-building power.

FACT!

How Many Calories?

People need various daily amounts of calories, depending on how old and how physically active they are. Boys usually need more than girls. Food scientists figure that an average person needs about 2,000 calories a day—with more than half of all the calories coming from carbohydrates. But it's not just about how many calories we get. The most important thing is to have a healthy balanced diet.

Nutrition Facts
Serving Size 1/4 Cup (30g)
Servings Per Container About 38

Amount Per Serving

alories 200 Calories from Fat 150

% Daily Value*

Fat 17g   26%

Fat 2.5g   13

Simple Carbs

Simple carbs are sugars. There are several kinds of sugars. Sucrose comes from sugar cane or sugar beets. You might spoon this from the sugar bowl and sprinkle it on your cereal. Fructose is a sugar in fruits and vegetables. Lactose, which is milk sugar, is found in cow's milk. Glucose is a sugar that circulates in the blood of animals. Guess what? Glucose is also called blood sugar. The body makes glucose from other carbohydrates. There are also large amounts of glucose in honey, grapes, and figs.

All fruits are rich in fructose, an energy-giving natural sugar.

When animals move, they draw upon the stores of glycogen in their body for energy.

Complex Carbs

Complex carbs are starch, cellulose, and glycogen. Starch and cellulose are the carbs that you eat in your food. Plants such as corn, potatoes, rice, and wheat store energy as starch. Your body can easily digest starch. Cellulose makes up the walls of plant cells and the fiber found in food. Your body cannot digest cellulose. Fiber is good because it helps your body get rid of waste from your large intestine.

You store energy as glycogen. Any extra carbohydrates that do not get used right away for energy get stored in the body as glycogen.

15

Sniffing Molecules

Certain molecules give foods their smells. When the molecules from a food enter your nose, you can smell the scent of the food. This experiment shows how molecules carry smells.

You will need:
- 1 orange
- 1 lemon
- 2 small bowls
- Grater
- A friend
- Scarf (as blindfold)

1. Grate some orange peel into a bowl.
2. Grate some lemon peel into the other bowl.

3. Blindfold your friend.
4. Let your friend smell each bowl. Ask him or her which smells like orange and which smells like lemon.
5. Change over, so you repeat the experiment.
6. What do you think gives lemons and oranges their smells?

Answer: Grating the lemon and orange sent some of their molecules into the air. You smelled special kinds of molecules called mirror molecules. The molecules that make up oranges and lemons contain the exact same atoms. The difference is that the atoms in lemon and orange molecules have the exact opposite arrangements. They are mirror images of each other in the same way that your right hand is the mirror image of your left hand.

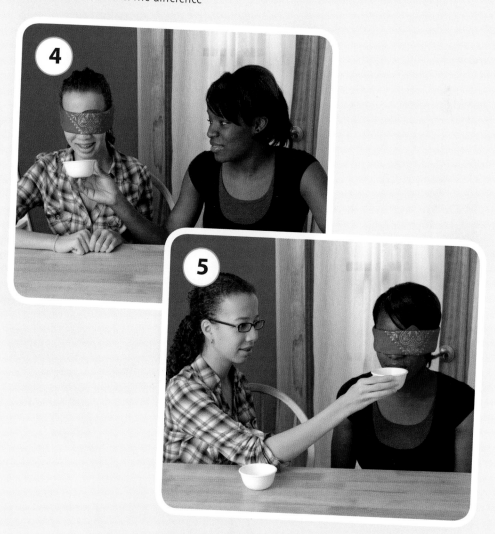

What Do Vitamins Do?

Your body is like a high-tech chemistry lab. Reactions happen all the time—as the cells in your body convert food to energy and repair your tissues. Vitamins help regulate those reactions. There are 13 vitamins, and you need small amounts of all of them to stay healthy. The vitamins have alphabetical names, such as vitamin A, vitamin C, and vitamin K. The 13 vitamins form two basic groups. They either dissolve in water or they dissolve in fats.

Imagine your body is a busy chemistry lab where lots of complicated chemical reactions take place. It takes a lot of vitamins to keep all those reactions bubbling away!

Dissolving in Water

Vitamin C and a group of eight B complex vitamins dissolve in water. Your body cannot store water-soluble vitamins. So you need to get them from food every day. Eating an orange can help supply your body with vitamin C. Other citrus fruits, along with cantaloupe, strawberries, and tomatoes, are all excellent sources of vitamin C. The B vitamins, numbers B_1, B_2, B_3, B_5, B_6, B_7, B_9, and B_{12}, play important roles in body processes such as growth and converting carbs to energy. Vitamin B_{12} and vitamin B_9 (folic acid) help make DNA—the master molecule of life. DNA directs all the workings of your cells. You get B vitamins by eating various fruits and vegetables. Meat, nuts, and whole grains are also rich in some B vitamins.

FACT!

Super Tomato

Not only is the humble tomato packed full of vitamins and minerals, it also contains antioxidants— chemicals that can help prevent or slow down damage to the cells in your body. Tomatoes are so good for you that some nutritionists call them a superfood.

DNA—and therefore all life—would be impossible without minerals and vitamins. Now do you realize how important they are in your diet?!

Dissolving in Fat

Vitamins A, D, E, and K dissolve in fat. Your liver can store these fat-soluble vitamins. Because of this, you don't need to eat these vitamins every day.

How do I keep my bones, teeth, and eyes healthy? Let's start with vitamin A. Vitamin A comes from animal products, including liver, meat, eggs, milk, and other dairy products. A chemical called carotene in some plants can make vitamin A. Carotene is in dark green leafy veggies, such as spinach, and orange veggies, such as carrots.

true tales

Mom! I'm Yellow!

In 1999 a child from Wales in the United Kingdom turned yellow after drinking too much orange juice. The 4-year-old girl drank more than 6 cups (1.5 liters) of the juice every day over many months. High levels of carotene, which converts to vitamin A in the body, are found in fruits such as oranges and cantaloupes and also in carrots. But having too much can turn you the same color as these foods! The girl returned to her normal color after cutting down on the amount she drank.

Stay fit and healthy by ensuring your diet is rich in essential vitamins.

Too much sun can cause skin cancer and burns, but a little sunshine helps your body make vitamin D.

Get some vitamin D!

Vitamin D keeps your teeth and bones healthy. This vitamin works with the minerals calcium and phosphorus to make and keep bones strong. Vitamin D is called the sunshine vitamin—because when rays from the sun strike the skin, the body makes vitamin D. Fish oil also contains vitamin D.

Vitamin E keeps your cell membranes healthy. You get vitamin E by eating wheat germ and whole grain foods. Vitamin E also comes from oils made from sunflower seeds and other seeds and vegetables.

If you cut your finger, vitamin K will help your blood to clot. Clotting stops your body from losing too much blood. You can get vitamin K by eating cauliflower and such leafy green veggies as cabbage, kale, and spinach.

What Do Minerals Do?

Minerals, like vitamins, take part in chemical reactions inside your body. Calcium, magnesium, potassium, sodium, iodine, iron, and zinc are minerals. Food scientists call them trace elements because your body needs only tiny amounts of minerals.

Iron forms a molecule in blood that carries oxygen around the body. Iodine helps keep the thyroid gland healthy. Some trace elements come from fruits and vegetables. Plant roots take up minerals in soil and water. By eating the plants, you take the minerals into your body. Milk is rich in the mineral calcium. We get sodium from table salt.

If you don't get enough iron in your diet, you may become anemic. This is a condition that makes people feel extremely tired all the time.

You Wouldn't Want Scurvy

In the 1400s and 1500s, sailors on long voyages often came down with a disease called scurvy. Their mouths became sore and their gums bled. Sometimes their teeth fell out. They bruised very easily, and if they cut themselves, the wound would not heal. Many sailors died from scurvy. In the mid-1700s, a doctor found that eating citrus fruits prevented the disease. A lack of vitamin C causes scurvy. It is one of many serious diseases caused by not getting enough vitamins.

FACT!

Build It Up

It is very important to eat a diet rich in calcium all of your life. In children and teens, calcium helps build strong bones and teeth. In older people, especially women, calcium can help prevent osteoporosis—a condition in which bones become weak and break easily.

Limes are rich in vitamin C. Ship captains packed their ships with the fruit to keep their crews healthy and free of scurvy.

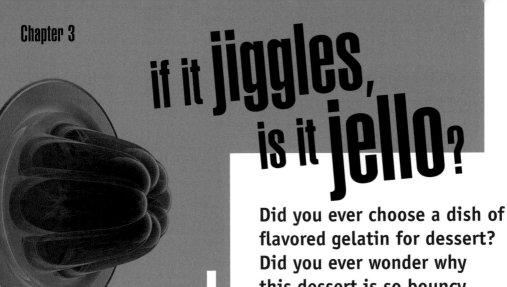

if it **jiggles,** is it **jello?**

Did you ever choose a dish of flavored gelatin for dessert? Did you ever wonder why this dessert is so bouncy and wiggly? You are about to unlock the secrets of gelatin.

It's Just a Phase

I'll bet you've heard adults say about a teen, "She is just going through a phase." They mean that the teen is in a stage of life that will change as time goes on. Solids, liquids, and gases are three states of matter. Scientists also call states of matter "phases."

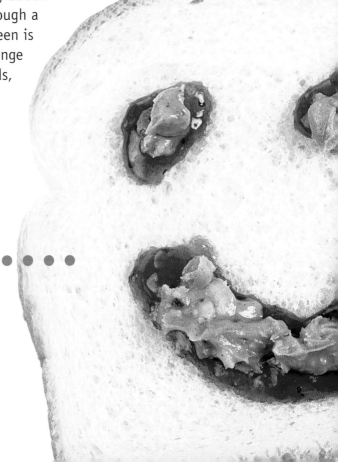

• • • • • • • • • • • • • • •

Take a look at this peanut butter and jelly sandwich—which part is a colloid? Read on!

A substance, such as water, can exist in all of the phases at various times. Water is usually a liquid, but it can also be solid ice or a gas called water vapor. What state a material is in usually depends upon its temperature. Higher temperatures turn liquids into gases. Lower temperatures turn liquids into solids.

How do you explain gelatin? It looks like a solid but moves around like a liquid. And what phase is mayonnaise? You can't shape it into a cube like a real solid. But when the Lunch Lady spreads it on a sandwich, it does not run off as a liquid would. The answer is: Jello and mayo are colloids. That is not as scary as it sounds. A colloid is simply a mixture of two or more substances that do not normally mix together. Many tiny bits of one material are scattered throughout another material to form a colloid. The materials that make up colloids are solids, liquids, or gases. There are also several types of colloids. Common types of colloids found in foods are called gels, emulsions, and foams.

FACT!

Solid or Liquid?

You can eat chocolate as a solid or drink it as a liquid—it tastes just as good in either form! If you melt a bar of chocolate in a pan, you'll see it change its state into a liquid form. If you put the pan in the fridge and leave it for a while, when you return you'll see the chocolate has changed state again, into a solid.

The Secret of Gelatin

Gelatin dessert is an example of a gel. A gel is a semisolid—a colloid made up of solid particles scattered in a liquid. Gelatin dessert starts out as powder in a box. The powder is made of cherry, strawberry, lemon, or another fruity flavoring, sweeteners, and collagen, a protein. Collagen helps hold together the skin, bones, and other tissues in animals. Under a powerful microscope, a molecule of collagen looks a bit like three spaghetti strands twisted together. What is the magic ingredient that turns collagen and fruity flavorings into a favorite dessert? Water.

Look at me now!

In its liquid form, gelatin can be poured into a mold. As the gelatin cools, the collagen molecules join together and the gelatin takes the shape of the mold.

About 87 percent of milk is water.

The Lunch Lady makes the dessert by mixing gelatin powder with hot water. First the hot water makes the collagen molecules come apart. They dissolve in the hot water. At this point the gelatin is a liquid. But as the water starts to cool, the collagen molecules try to go back to their original solid, twisted-spaghetti shape. But they can't. The collagen molecules come together in new ways. As they become solid particles, they form hollow places or pockets that trap water. The trapped water and those spaghetti-like collagen molecules are why gelatin is so jiggly.

Pass the Emulsion, Please

An emulsion is a colloid made from very small droplets of one liquid evenly scattered throughout another liquid. Milk is a food emulsion that includes liquid butterfat globules in liquid water. Butterfat is also called milk fat. Butter, cream, margarine, and mayonnaise are similar kinds of emulsions.

Fear of Water

You may have heard the saying "Water and oil do not mix." Think of salad dressings. Made of vinegar and oil, they are emulsions of oil particles suspended in vinegar. Vinegar is a watery liquid. Oil will not mix with watery vinegar. As in all other emulsions, they do not mix because the oil and water molecules "ignore" each other. They stay separate from each other. Why do salad dressing labels say "shake well before using?" You have to shake up the watery vinegar and oil, because otherwise they would just stay separate.

Let's Stick Together

Mayonnaise has three parts: oil, vinegar or lemon juice, and egg yolks. As with salad dressing, the oil and vinegar do not mix. Adding egg yolks fixes this. The egg yolk contains a chemical that acts as an emulsifier, which is like a go-between. Emulsifiers are part water-fearing molecules and part water-loving molecules. Emulsifiers attach to both the oil and water molecules and keep them from separating.

Oil + vinegar or lemon juice + egg yolk = mayo.

FACT!

The Fourth State

Solids, liquids, and gases are the three best-known states of matter. Colloids are so important, however, that some scientists call them the "fourth state of matter."

Other Yummy Colloids

Marshmallows and the topping on lemon meringue pie are colloids called foams. Foams are made of gas bubbles in liquids or solids. Cooks make meringue for pies by whipping together egg whites and other ingredients. The whipping creates air bubbles in the egg whites to produce a foamy meringue.

Marshmallow is a colloid foam of gas in a solid. The gas is air. The solid is made from combining sugar, corn syrup, and gelatin dissolved in hot water. Whipping the combined ingredients creates air bubbles. When the ingredients cool, the result is marshmallow foam.

When you toast marshmallows, you force the collagen molecules in them to separate—this makes the marshmallows soft and gooey.

How to Make Colloid Dough

When you were younger, you may have had fun shaping play dough. Play dough is a colloid, just as milk and lemon meringue are. In fact, pie crust is a colloid similar to play dough. You can make this simple colloid:

You will need:
- 1 cup cornstarch
- 1 bowl
- 1 spoon
- Water
- Plate or pan

1. Place 1 cup of cornstarch into the bowl.

2. Use the spoon to stir in small amounts of water until the mixture begins to thicken.

3. Pour the mixture onto the plate or pan.
4. Scoop some up in your hand and squeeze it.

Can you guess why your colloid dough is both like a liquid and a solid and also like neither?

Answer: The cornstarch does not dissolve in water. The cornstarch particles remain suspended in the water. The dough is a colloid made up of solid cornstarch particles in liquid water. It behaves like a semisolid.

4

why is that chicken gray?

What sort of food is that? The Lunch Lady may have signs telling you the grayish stuff is chicken and the orange stuff is sweet potato. But there are other clues to food. Your eyes tell you the red sauce is for spaghetti. Your nose smells the delicious scent of apple pie. What makes those wonderful sights and smells? The answer is cooking.

From Campfires to Kitchens

Who first came up with the idea of cooking? Archaeologists find out about ancient people and places by digging up where they once lived—and looking for clues. But they are not sure where or how people first learned to cook food.

Smells great!

When you bake an apple pie, the heat from the oven creates chemical reactions in the food—and one of the results is that freshly baked apple pie smell.

Early people had no fire—and no Lunch Lady—so there was no choice but to eat the meat from hunted animals raw!

People used to eat meat just as they found it—raw. Scientists suspect that the first cooked dinners happened by accident. Imagine a terrible forest fire in prehistoric times that killed many animals. Perhaps ancient people sampled the meat from the burned animals and found it much tastier than raw meat.

The first deliberate use of fire is another discovery that was lost in time. But early people in Africa and China may have used fire to cook as many as 1 million years ago. In Europe people used fire to cook at least 125,000 years ago. About 10,000 years ago, people in today's Middle East region learned how to farm. They discovered how to grow grain and how to raise animals for food. Ancient people built ovens for baking bread and made pots for cooking soups and stews.

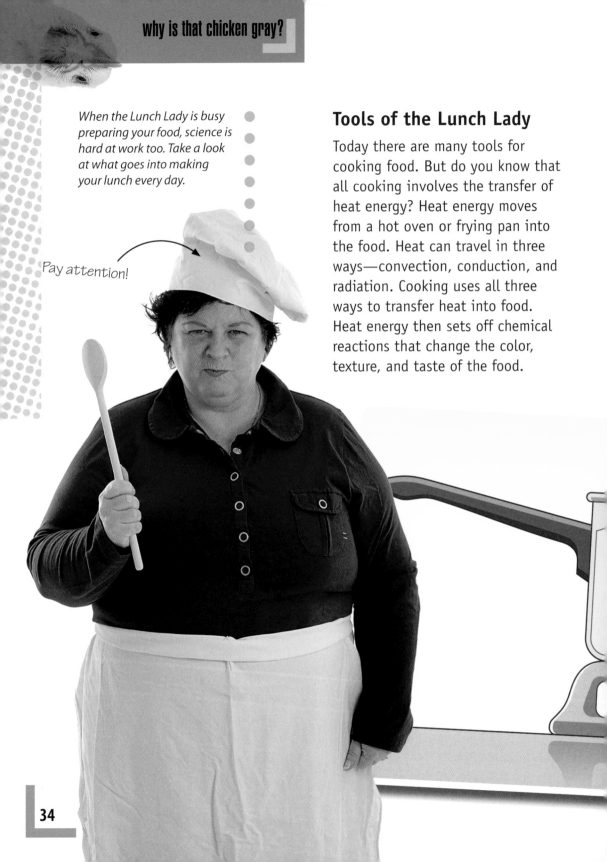

When the Lunch Lady is busy preparing your food, science is hard at work too. Take a look at what goes into making your lunch every day.

Pay attention!

Tools of the Lunch Lady

Today there are many tools for cooking food. But do you know that all cooking involves the transfer of heat energy? Heat energy moves from a hot oven or frying pan into the food. Heat can travel in three ways—convection, conduction, and radiation. Cooking uses all three ways to transfer heat into food. Heat energy then sets off chemical reactions that change the color, texture, and taste of the food.

Hot Air and Hot Water

Convection transfers heat to food by the movement of a heated gas or liquid around the food. All ovens transfer heat by convection. The heated material is a gas—the air inside the oven. An electric coil or gas burner heats the air around it. The hot air flows toward cooler air in other places inside the oven. This movement of hot to cooler air is called a convection current. To roast meat, such as beef and chicken, or vegetables, the Lunch Lady slides the food into a hot oven. Roasting is a way of cooking that turns food brown. The oven temperature must be above 400°F (205°C) to start the chemical reactions that turn meat or vegetables brown. The Lunch Lady also uses convection in an oven to bake bread, muffins, or pizza. Convection moves the air in an oven from the heat source to the food being cooked. At the point of contact with the food, heat then travels by conduction.

Convection in a deep fryer cooks fried chicken or french fries. A deep fryer is a pot filled with hot oil. The movement of convection currents in the oil transfers heat energy to pieces of raw potatoes or chicken. Convection currents in a pot of water can boil many foods, such as potatoes and other vegetables. At the point of contact with the food, heat again travels by conduction.

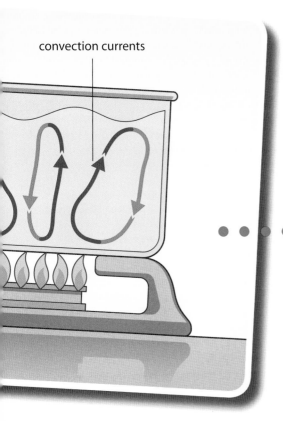

convection currents

Heat energy is transferred from boiling water to the food within it when food is cooked in a pot.

Hot Metal

So what's conduction all about? Conduction is the movement of heat through a material. Metals are some of the best conductors of heat energy. A metal frying pan is a conduction tool found in all kitchens. A gas flame or an electric coil heats the metal of the pan. The atoms and molecules in the pan move faster and faster. They collide with atoms and molecules of anything touching the pan. The Lunch Lady throws some sliced onions into a hot pan. Mmm ... The atoms and molecules in the onions begin to move faster as heat energy moves into them by conduction. What happens next? The food starts cooking, releasing delicious smells.

Radiant Heat

Radiation carries heat energy across empty space. The movement of atoms and molecules in any object gives off rays of radiation called infrared rays. The hotter an object is, the more infrared rays it gives off. Infrared rays from the sun warm Earth. Closer to your school lunchroom, broilers, grills, and microwave ovens are tools that cook foods by radiation. Hot grills or broilers give off infrared rays. Microwave ovens give off microwaves. Energy from this radiation causes atoms and molecules in objects it strikes to move faster. This movement produces heat energy that causes fish to broil, steaks to grill, and microwave popcorn to pop.

You have atoms and molecules to thank for that bacon and egg breakfast! They crashed and smashed together to cook the food into a great-tasting meal.

Energy radiates from the sun and travels 93 million miles (149 million kilometers) through space to reach Earth.

Why Beef Is Brown and Chicken Is Not

When prehistoric people cooked the red meat from mammoths and saber-toothed cats, it probably looked as roast beef does today. Early people roasted animals over an open fire. Roasting sets off a series of chemical reactions that change the color, texture, and flavor of red meat.

In 1912 a French scientist named Louis Camille Maillard explained why cooked beef and other red meats turn brown. Raw meat contains protein and sugar, such as glucose. The protein is made up of amino acids. Heat makes the sugar and amino acids in red meat break down into new chemicals. The chemicals react with one another over and over, creating a lovely brown color. Together these complex reactions are called the Maillard Reaction, named for the French scientist who first explained them. Other foods, such as bread or bagels, also turn brown. Poultry and other white meats do not contain as much sugar as red meat, so they do not turn as dark.

FACT!

Microwaves

Microwave ovens are cooking tools that create short, high-energy waves. These waves strike mainly water molecules in food and cause them to vibrate very fast. The vibrating water molecules transfer heat energy throughout the food.

Inventing the Microwave

The microwave oven was invented by accident. Percy Spencer, an engineer for a company in Massachusetts, was working on a project in 1946 with a piece of equipment called a magnetron. While standing near the magnetron, he noticed that a candy bar in his pocket started to melt. He knew that the magnetron gave off microwaves. Were the microwaves melting the chocolate? He tested this idea with popcorn and then with an egg. The popcorn popped, but he ended up with egg on his face, quite literally! Spencer went on to develop the popular microwave oven.

What Makes It Hot?

Heat is a form of energy. It comes from the movement of tiny particles, called atoms and molecules, that make up all objects. Atoms and molecules are always moving around. When they move slowly, the object is cool. So the atoms in an ice cube are moving very slowly.

When atoms and molecules move quickly, the object is warm or hot. Fast-moving atoms and molecules crash into other atoms and molecules and make them move faster. Atoms and molecules in a hot frying pan or pot of boiling oil are moving around very quickly.

Inside each kernel of popcorn is a tiny amount of water. When the popcorn is heated, the water starts to boil and release steam. The steam pressure inside the kernel builds and builds until the kernel can contain it no longer—and it POPS!

Trick of Invisible Ink

You can use some liquids as invisible ink. When the "ink" dries, the message disappears. How can you make the message reappear? Try this experiment to find out:

You will need:
- Cotton swab
- Orange juice
- Paper
- Toaster

1. Moisten a cotton swab with orange juice.
2. Use the swab as a pen to write your name on paper in orange juice.

3. Let the paper dry and watch your name disappear.
4. Turn on the toaster and let it heat up.

5. Ask an adult to hold the paper just above the toaster. Take care because the toaster could set the paper on fire.
6. Observe how heat makes your invisible name appear.

What do you think causes orange juice to function as invisible ink?

Answer: The reaction that causes your name to reappear is called the Maillard Reaction. Orange juice contains lots of sugar and some protein. The browning caused by the Maillard Reaction changes the color of the orange juice ink when the paper gets hot.

where did this stuff come from?

Sometimes the food spooned onto your plate can look mighty mysterious. How about some little green balls in white goo? The Lunch Lady calls them creamed peas. How did they start, though? Well, there's no real mystery about where food comes from in the lunchroom or anywhere else. Everything that lands on your plate comes from the sun.

FACT!

The Chain Gang

Plants form the base of a long chain of organisms that make up a food chain. Plants are producers—organisms that provide food for other organisms within the food chain. The entire chain relies upon producers—larger organisms, such as sheep, eat them for energy, and in turn these organisms are then eaten by other organisms, such as humans, higher up in the food chain. If a "link" in the food chain is broken at any point, it affects every organism in the chain.

Unlike animals, plants do not need to get their food from other organisms.

The Sun and Creamed Peas

The sun provides energy for all life on Earth. Everything that shows up on your lunch plate was once alive. The flow of energy that produces the food you eat begins with the sun. The sun's energy gets stored in green plants. Peas come from plants.

Unlike people, plants do not have to stand in a line and wait for lunch. Plants make their own food by using carbon dioxide gas from air, water taken up by roots, and the energy in sunlight. This is called photosynthesis. Organisms that make their own food are producers.

Chlorophyll, a green pigment in the cells of plant leaves, takes in light rays. Cell parts called chloroplasts contain the chlorophyll. Chloroplasts are like mini chemistry labs. Complex chemical reactions go on inside these chloroplasts. Water molecules—made of oxygen and hydrogen atoms—get split apart. The hydrogen combines with carbon dioxide to make a simple sugar. Green plants use these ingredients, along with minerals taken from the soil, to create starch, vegetable fat, vitamins, and other nutrients that people and other animals need for growth and health.

Growing Garden Cress from Seeds

See photosynthesis in action by growing garden cress from its seeds.

You will need:
- Shallow tray
- Paper towels
- Jug of water
- Packet of garden cress seeds
- Pair of scissors

1. Line the shallow tray with two or three sheets of paper towels.

2. Slowly pour water onto the paper towels. You don't need too much— just enough to soak them.

3. Sprinkle the garden cress seeds over the paper towels.

4. Leave the tray on a sunny windowsill.

5. Check the seeds every few days to make sure the paper towels do not dry out.

6. After a couple of weeks, the garden cress plants should be fully grown. Harvest your plants with a pair of sharp scissors. Wash the garden cress and use it as a sandwich filler or as a garnish.

Garden cress is one of the easiest plants to grow, but the seeds need plenty of water and sunlight. Repeat the experiment but sow the seeds on dry paper towels. What happens? Repeat the experiment again, sprinkling the seeds on soaked paper towels, but this time leave the tray in a dark place. How successful is your experiment?

Cream Sauce from Cows

The cream sauce for creamed peas contains butter and cream. These ingredients come from cow's milk. Cows and other animals cannot make their own food. Cows live in green pastures and eat grass.

Organisms that cannot make their own food are consumers. They must eat food. All animals, including people, are consumers. They eat plants and animals that eat plants. Some consumers also eat animals that eat other animals. The energy that first came to producers from the sun gets passed along through consumers.

Cows eat plants for energy. Humans in turn eat the meat of cows and drink their milk for energy. In this food chain, the plant is the producer, the cow is the primary consumer, and the human is the secondary consumer.

Modern farming relies upon the use of large machinery, such as combines, to harvest huge quantities of grain for food.

Food from Farms

Fruits and vegetables come from gardens, farms, and orchards. Most meat comes from ranches or farms. Fishing boats bring in fish and seafood.

Before people learned to grow food, they fished and hunted wild animals. These early people roamed from place to place, gathering nuts, berries, and other food from wild plants. Once people learned to grow plants and raise animals, they settled down. From then on, people got most of their food through raising animals and growing crops. With the invention of modern machinery, farming became a huge industry. Scientists developed ways to grow food more efficiently. They bred high-producing plants and animals. They developed chemicals to help crops grow and kill weeds and insect pests.

Today farming provides grains, vegetables, meat, poultry, eggs, milk, and other dairy products to people all over the world.

Choosing Organic Food

Some people worry that chemicals used to grow plants and raise livestock can be harmful to humans who eat them. Organic foods offer an alternative. These foods are grown without chemical weed or pest killers. Organic meat and animal products come from animals that have not been treated with chemicals such as hormones.

how old is this pickle?

Some of the food grown on farms comes straight to stores and school lunchrooms. You can find fresh lettuce, tomatoes, cucumbers, and other vegetables in a salad. Try a fresh apple or orange for a healthy dessert. Much of the food produced by modern farming, however, takes a detour to a food-processing plant. These plants are big food factories. They often preserve foods so that they can be kept longer.

Food from Cans and Jars

Now don't get scared, but that bowl of chicken noodle soup you ate for lunch might be more than a year old. But that's OK. Soup, stewed tomatoes, pickles, cooked fruits, and many other lunchroom foods may be canned, either in cans or in glass jars. Canning keeps food from spoiling by heating it and then sealing it in the cans or jars.

true tales

Beryl, Les, and a Very Old Chicken

When Beryl and Les married in 1956, they received a food hamper as a gift. Les promised to eat one item, a can of chicken, on their 50th wedding anniversary. In 2006 he kept his promise. Les, an ex-soldier, was not afraid of a can of old chicken. He made sure the chicken was well heated through before eating it. Food experts said that it was safe for Les to eat the chicken as long as it had been stored correctly and canned properly at high temperatures and high pressure, and the can was free from bumps. Les, age 73, felt fine after eating the chicken. So canned food can last for a long time if stored and prepared in the correct way.

Preserving food in cans and jars is one of the greatest food inventions of modern times. It allows people to harvest food in large quantities, then store it for when they need it later.

The secret to canning is knowing how hot is hot enough. High temperatures kill microbes in food. Some people can at home by putting fruits, jams and jellies, or tomatoes in jars and heating the jars in boiling water, which is 212°F (100°C). But that's not hot enough for other foods. Jars or cans of mushrooms, vegetables, and meats must be heated to at least 240°F (116°C). A poison could grow in canned mushrooms, vegetables, and meats unless the cans are pressure heated. This toxin causes a type of food poisoning called botulism. It attacks the nervous system and can paralyze muscles.

Canning also uses airtight seals. A vacuum forms, stopping air from getting back inside the jar and adding more microbes. In food-processing plants, machines fill cans or jars on conveyor belts. The cans and jars move to areas hot enough to kill germs, where the containers are tightly sealed.

The world's super freezer!

The Arctic acts as a giant freezer, perfectly preserving anything that falls into its ice.

Fresh or Frozen?

Thanks to an invention of Charles Birdseye in the early 1900s, those peas that the Lunch Lady served may once have been frozen. Birdseye was working as a fur trader in the Arctic when he saw that fish thrown on the ice froze quickly as the winter wind blew over them. When they thawed, the fish tasted just as fresh as when they had been caught. Birdseye found that the less time it took fish, or any food, to freeze, the better it tasted when thawed. Using this observation, Birdseye invented a technique called quick freezing or flash freezing.

Imagine a world without freezers! Thanks to Birdseye, we can eat fish that is weeks old, and it still tastes (and smells) good.

Frozen Peas

Did you know that freezing is a great way to preserve foods? Meats, vegetables, and fruits spoil because microscopic organisms grow rapidly in them. At temperatures below 0°F (−18°C), these microbes grow very slowly or not at all. Food processors quickly freeze individual peas, other vegetables, and fruits by blasting them with ice cold air. Quick freezing stops the cell walls in the food from breaking down and forming big ice crystals. So quick freezing keeps the color, flavor, and nutrients of food better than regular freezing.

Food processors quickly freeze boxed foods, such as pizza, by pressing the box between two freezing plates. Quick-frozen hamburger patties and hot dogs travel by conveyor belt down a tunnel filled with vaporized liquid gas, such as nitrogen. Canned juice or sealed packages of shrimp or cooked dishes get quick-frozen by sending them on a conveyor belt through an icy cold liquid. Remember the creamed peas? A food-processing plant may have created huge vats of them, sealed small batches in bags, and quickly frozen them. All the Lunch Lady had to do was thaw them and heat them.

Food processing has changed the way we eat today. Fast food, such as hot dogs, has become a quick and cheap food supply.

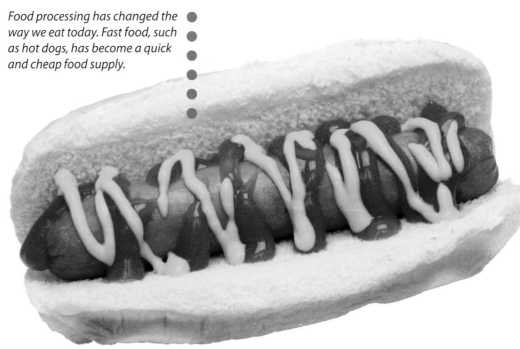

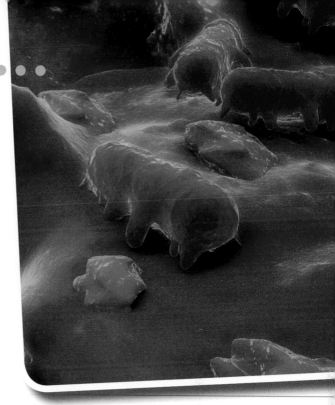

Bacteria are found everywhere, but some forms are extremely dangerous and can cause illness or even death if they enter the digestive system.

Slicing Lunchmeat

Meat processing is a huge food industry. At big processing plants, butchers slice up meat into steaks and roasts and grind beef into hamburger. They make bacon, sausages, lunchmeat, and hot dogs. They cut up chickens into wings, thighs, and breasts.

Keeping workspaces clean and germ-free is important for all food-processing plants. It is especially important for meat processing. Many different microbes grow in raw meat. Some animals also carry germs in their bodies. Chickens can carry *Salmonella* bacteria, which can be spread through chicken waste. *Salmonella* produce a toxin that causes abdominal pain, nausea, and diarrhea in humans.

The ceilings, floors, walls, and work tables in meat-processing plants must be washed with germ-killing cleaners. Clothing must also be clean. Inspectors check the meat at various stages of processing to be sure it is germ-free.

FACT!

Soap and Water

After meat and other foods leave the food-processing plant, you can help keep them germ-free. The most important thing is to wash your hands with soap and water before and after handling food. Be sure that any meat you eat is cooked thoroughly. Never put cooked chicken or other meat on a plate that held the raw meat.

Watering Beans

One way to store some foods for long periods of time is to dry them by removing any water in them. Removing water is called dehydration. Putting the water back is called rehydration. Beans are one of the most popular foods that can be dried and stored. Dried beans are often rehydrated and used in bean soup or chili. Just how much water can various kinds of dried beans soak up? Find out by doing this experiment:

You will need:
- 3 kinds of dried beans (e.g., pinto beans, kidney beans, and lima beans)
- 3 12-ounce plastic cups
- Permanent marker
- Water
- Measuring cup
- Strainer
- Food scale
- Plastic wrap
- Paper towel
- Writing paper (to record results)

1. Create a chart that looks like this:

Type of bean	Dehydrated weight	Rehydrated weight
Pinto		
Kidney		
Lima		

2. Select three of each type of bean and weigh the three beans on a food scale.

3. Record the dehydrated weight of each type of bean on the chart.

4. Place three beans in each cup. Use one cup for pinto beans, one for kidney beans, and one for lima beans.

5. Use the permanent marker to label each cup with the name of the beans.

6. Pour 10 ounces of water into each cup.

7. Cover the cups and let them stand for 24 hours.

8. Pour the water and beans from one cup into a strainer. Carefully pat the excess water off the beans with a paper towel.

9. Weigh the three beans on a food scale. Record the rehydrated weight on the chart.

10. Repeat with the other two cups of beans.

Are the weights of each type of bean the same or different? If they are different, figure out why. Some types of bean can absorb more water than others.

when i swallow, where does it go?

That macaroni and cheese the Lunch Lady served tastes great. As you chew it, your taste buds pick up all the delicious flavors. Then you swallow it. Now what? How do macaroni and cheese, fruits and vegetables, burgers, and spaghetti turn into fuel that your body can use? The answer is digestion. This process breaks down food into smaller parts. There are several steps to digestion.

Step 1: Chewing

As soon as you put food into your mouth, digestion begins. Chewing gets things started. Your teeth grind the food into smaller pieces. At the same time, saliva in your mouth mixes with the ground-up food. This turns your food into a slimy, pasty ball. It is now ready to slide down a tube called the esophagus into your stomach.

Taking a bite of food is just the start of the digestive process—that bite now has to travel the entire way through your digestive system.

Breaking Down Bread

This experiment is so simple all you need is a slice of white bread — and your mouth to chew it!

> You will need:
> - Slice of white bread

1. Put half a slice of white bread into your mouth.
2. Chew the bread. Keep on chewing the bread. Don't swallow… keep on munching on the bread for about five minutes.
3. Pay close attention to the flavor of the bread. Do you notice any changes?
4. When you think you've got the answer, you can swallow the mush in your mouth … or spit it out!

Bread is made up of complex molecules called starch, which consists of long chains of sugar (glucose) molecules. As you chew the bread, the saliva in your mouth starts to break up the starch into sugars. At this point you should notice that the bready mush in your mouth tastes slightly sweet. The saliva has started to digest the bread.

Step 2: Churning

Your stomach is a bag of muscles. The job of the stomach muscles is to churn that pasty ball and break it down some more. A powerful acid called gastric juice digests protein in cheese, meat, eggs, and milk. Churning turns food in the stomach into chyme, which is a thick liquid. Chyme then pours into the next part of the digestive system, called the small intestine.

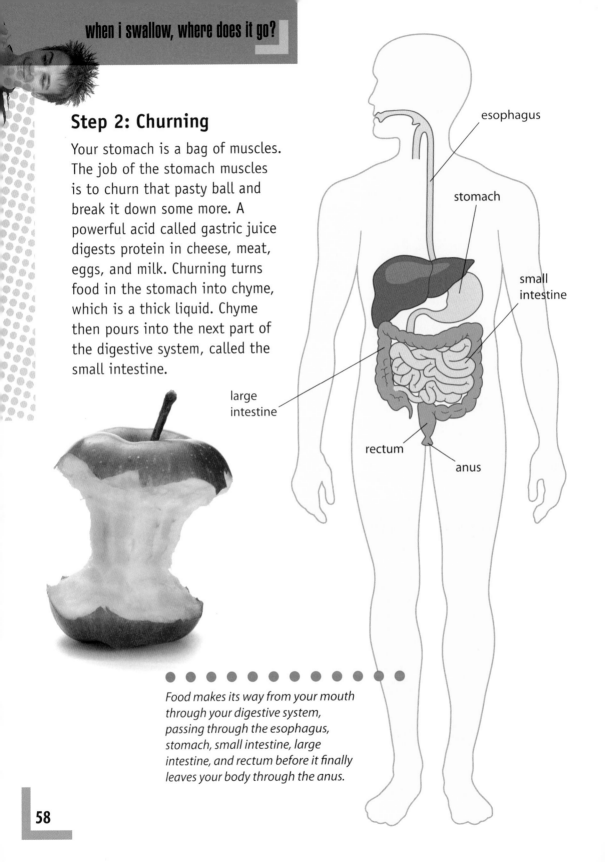

esophagus

stomach

small intestine

large intestine

rectum

anus

Food makes its way from your mouth through your digestive system, passing through the esophagus, stomach, small intestine, large intestine, and rectum before it finally leaves your body through the anus.

Step 3: Complete Breakdown

In the small intestine, food gets totally broken down into all its chemical parts. A mixture of juices from an organ called the pancreas and from the wall of the small intestine breaks protein into amino acids. These juices finish breaking carbohydrates into the simple sugar glucose. The liver produces bile. This substance breaks up large fat molecules into chemicals called fatty acids and a substance called cholesterol.

Amino acids, sugar, and fatty acids then pass through the walls of the small intestine and into a network of blood vessels. Water, minerals, and vitamins also leave the small intestine in this way. Blood carries the nutrients to cells and organs throughout the body.

Step 4: Getting Rid of Waste

The small intestine cannot digest all parts of food. The unused parts are called waste, which moves to the large intestine. The large intestine soaks up water and some vitamins and minerals from waste. Fiber that cannot be digested helps the body get rid of waste. The waste passes through the rectum and anus and out of the body.

The restroom is the end of the incredible journey that food makes through your body!

A Long Journey

The energy that makes your body work travels an amazing pathway. It begins with the rays of sunlight that plants use to make food from water and carbon dioxide. This energy, stored as carbohydrates in plants, passes to humans and animals that eat the plants. Energy is stored in animals and animal products, mainly as protein and fat. The Lunch Lady dishes up that stored energy, along with vitamins and minerals that help keep you healthy. The energy makes that amazing journey from the sun, through the Lunch Lady, to you.

FACT!

Fighting Cancers

Substances in food called antioxidants may stop some kinds of cancer and other diseases. Antioxidants help prevent damage to tissues when your body burns food. Oranges and other foods rich in vitamin C are powerful antioxidants. Berries, nuts, carrots, spinach, and other leafy green vegetables are also good sources of antioxidants.

Now you know what you need to eat to give you endless energy. Make sure you put more than pizza on your plate when you eat your next lunch!

Thanks, Lunch Lady!

Dinosaur Bones

It's not good to play with your food, but sometimes it's OK to study it. Could that chicken on your lunch plate be the descendant of a dinosaur? This idea is not some wild science fiction idea. Many scientists believe that birds evolved from certain kinds of dinosaurs. In fact, scientists have found evidence that chickens evolved from the ferocious tyrannosaurus rex. They found that the bones of chickens and dinosaurs have similar shapes. They studied chemicals in the dinosaur bones and found substances similar to those in chicken bones. You can see for yourself. Ask the Lunch Lady or a cook in your family or neighborhood to save you the skeleton of a chicken.

1. Boil the bones in water and scrape them to remove any leftover meat.
2. Soak the bones in bleach to kill germs.
3. Dry the bones with the paper towels and put them together.
4. Look at pictures of t-rex bones.

Write down your observations: How do you think chicken and dinosaur bones are the same or different? How does this support or disprove the idea that birds descended from dinosaurs?

You will need:
● Bones of a whole chicken
● Bleach
● Paper towels
● Diagram of tyrannosaurus rex skeleton
● Journal for recording your observations

glossary

amino acids—the chemical building blocks of proteins

arteries—blood vessels that carry blood around the body

carbohydrates—sugars, starch, and cellulose in food

chlorophyll—the green pigment in plant cells that captures energy from the sun

chloroplast—a plant cell part that contains chlorophyll

colloid—a mix made of two substances, one within another

conduction—heat transfer from a hot material to a cool one

convection—heat transfer in gases or liquids, as warmer parts rise and heat cooler parts

digestion—the process of breaking down food in the body

emulsion—a colloid made of droplets of one liquid scattered throughout another liquid

enzymes—special proteins that speed up chemical reactions in body cells

fats—greasy substances in animal bodies

foam—a colloid made of gas bubbles in a solid or liquid

hormones—special proteins that start processes in the body

intestine—the part of the digestive system between the stomach and anus

minerals—nonliving natural substances needed in small amounts for good nutrition

molecules—atoms linked together in a way that forms the smallest unit of a chemical substance

nutrient—a food substance needed for growth and life

obese—grossly overweight

photosynthesis—the process green plants use to make food from water and carbon dioxide

protein—large molecules made of amino acids that make up such body parts as muscle, hair, and hormones and must be eaten as food

radiation—the transfer of heat energy as electromagnetic waves

scurvy—disease caused by a lack of vitamin C

vacuum—a space that contains no matter

vitamins—nutrients; chemical compounds that are needed for good health

additional resources

Read More

Brasch, Nicolas. *The Foods We Eat*. North Mankato, Minn.:
  Smart Apple Media, 2010.

Reilly, Kathleen M. *Food: 25 Amazing Projects: Investigate
  the History and Science of What We Eat*. White River Junction,
  Vt.: Nomad Press, 2010.

Sohn, Emily, and Sarah Webb. *Food and Nutrition*. Broomall, Pa.:
  Chelsea Clubhouse, 2006.

Thornhill, Jan. *Who Wants Pizza?: The Kids' Guide to the History, Science
  and Culture of Food*. Toronto: Maple Tree Press, 2010.

Internet Sites

Use FactHound to find Internet sites related to this book.
All of the sites on FactHound have been researched by our staff.

Here's all you do:
Visit *www.facthound.com*
Type in this code:
9780756544843

index

About the author:
Darlene R. Stille has
combined her joint love of
science and writing in the
100 science books for young
readers she has written. She
lives and writes in Michigan.